oasis

(WHAT'S THE STORY) MORNING GLORY ?

WISE PUBLICATIONS
London / New York / Paris / Sydney / Copenhagen / Madrid

Exclusive Distributors:
Music Sales Limited
8/9 Frith Street, London W1V 5TZ, England.

Music Sales Pty Limited
120 Rothschild Avenue, Rosebery, NSW 2018, Australia.

Order No.AM934802
ISBN 0-7119-5465-8
This book © Copyright 1995 by Wise Publications.

Book design by Michael Bell Design.
Music arranged by Arthur Dick.
Music processed by The Pitts.

Printed in the United Kingdom by
Caligraving Limited, Thetford, Norfolk.

Your Guarantee of Quality
As publishers, we strive to produce every
book to the highest commercial standards.
Whilst endeavouring to retain the original
running order of the recorded album, the book
has been carefully designed to minimise awkward
page turns and to make playing from it a real pleasure.
Particular care has been given to specifying acid-free,
neutral-sized paper made from pulps which
have not been elemental chlorine bleached.
This pulp is from farmed sustainable forests and
was produced with special regard for the environment.
Throughout, the printing and binding have been
planned to ensure a sturdy, attractive publication
which should give years of enjoyment.
If your copy fails to meet our high standards,
please inform us and we will gladly replace it.

Music Sales' complete catalogue describes thousands
of titles and is available in full colour sections by subject,
direct from Music Sales Limited.
Please state your areas of interest and send
a cheque/postal order for £1.50 for postage to:
Music Sales Limited, Newmarket Road,
Bury St. Edmunds, Suffolk IP33 3YB.

HELLO

I don't feel as if I know you
You take up all my time
The days are long and the night will throw you away
'Cause the sun don't shine

Nobody ever mentions the weather
Can make or break your day
Nobody ever seems to remember
Life is a game we play
We live in the shadows and we had the chance and threw it away

And it's never gonna be the same
'Cos the years are falling by the rain
It's never gonna be the same
'Til the light by you comes to my house and says hello

There ain't no sense in feeling lonely
They got no faith in you
But I've got a feeling you still owe me
So wipe the shit from your shoes

Nobody ever mentions the weather
Can make or break your day
Nobody ever seems to remember
Life is a game we play
We live in the shadows and we had the chance and threw it away

And it's never gonna be the same
'Cos the years are falling by the rain
It's never gonna be the same
'Til the light by you comes to my house and says

Hello, hello (it's good to be back, it's good to be back)
Hello, hello (it's good to be back, it's good to be back)
Hello, hello (it's good to be back, it's good to be back)
Hello, hello, hello

WONDERWALL

Today is gonna be the day
That they're gonna throw it back to you
By now you should have somehow
Realised what you gotta do
I don't believe that anybody feels the way that I do
About you now

Back beat, the word is on the street that the fire in your heart is out
I'm sure you've heard it all before but you never really had a doubt
I don't believe that anybody feels the way that I do about you now

And all the roads we have to walk are winding
And all the lights that lead us there are blinding
There are many things that I would like to say to you
But I don't know how

Because maybe you're gonna be the one that saves me
And after all you're my wonderwall

Today was gonna be the day
But they'll never throw it back to you
By now you should've somehow
Realised what you're not to do
I don't believe that anybody feels the way that I do
About you now

And all the roads that lead you there are winding
And all the lights that light the way are blinding
There are many things that I would like to say to you
But I don't know how

Because maybe you're gonna be the one that saves me
And after all you're my wonderwall

I said maybe you're gonna be the one that saves me
And after all you're my wonderwall

I said maybe you're gonna be the one that saves me
You're gonna be the one that saves me

ROLL WITH IT

You gotta roll with it, you gotta take your time
You gotta say what you say, don't let anybody get in your way
'Cause it's all too much for me to take

Don't ever stand aside, don't ever be denied
You wanna be who you'd be if you're comin' with me
I think I've got a feelin' I've lost inside
I think I'm gonna take me away and hide
I'm thinkin' of things that I just can't abide

I know the roads down which your life will drive
I'll find the key that lets you stop inside
Kiss the girl she's not behind the door
But you know I think I recognise your face
But I never seen you before

You gotta roll with it, you gotta take your time
You gotta say what you say, don't let anybody get in your way
'Cause it's all too much for me to take

I know the roads down which your life will drive
I'll find the key that lets you stop inside
Kiss the girl she's not behind the door
But you know I think I recognise your face
But I never seen you before

You gotta roll with it, you gotta take your time
You gotta say what you say, don't let anybody get in your way
'Cause it's all too much for me to take

Don't ever stand aside, don't ever be denied
You wanna be who you'd be if you're comin' with me
I think I've got a feelin' I've lost inside
I think I've got a feelin' I've lost inside

DON'T LOOK BACK IN ANGER

Slip inside the eye of your mind
Don't you know you might find a better place to play
You said that you never been
But all the things that you've seen slowly fade away

So I must start a revolution from my bed
'Cause you said the brains I had went to my head
Step outside, summertime's in bloom
Stand up beside the fireplace, take that look from off your face
You ain't ever gonna burn my heart out

And so Sally can wait, she knows it's too late
As we're walking on by
Her soul slides away,
But don't look back in anger, I heard you say

Take me to the place where you go
Where nobody knows if it's night or day
But please don't put your life in the hands
Of a rock'n'roll band who'll throw it all away

I'm gonna start a revolution from my bed
'Cause you said the brains I had went to my head
Step outside, 'cause summertime's in bloom
Stand up beside the fireplace, take that look from off your face
'Cause you ain't never gonna burn my heart out

And so Sally can wait, she knows it's too late
As we're walking on by
Her soul slides away,
But don't look back in anger, I heard you say

So Sally can wait, she knows it's too late
As we're walking on by
Her soul slides away,
But don't look back in anger, I heard you say

So Sally can wait, she knows it's too late
As we're walking on by
Her soul slides away,
But don't look back in anger,
Don't look back in anger I heard you say
It's not too late

HEY NOW

I hitched a ride with my soul by the side of the road
Just as the sky turned black
I took a walk with my fame down memory lane
I never did find my way back

You know that I gotta say time's slippin' away
What will it hold for me?
What am I gonna do while I'm lookin' at you?
You're standing ignoring me

I thought that I heard someone say now
There's no time for running away now
Hey now, hey now

Feel no shame
'Cause time's no chain
Feel no shame

The first thing I saw
As I walked through the door
Was a sign on the wall that read
It said you might never know
That I want you to know
What's written inside of your head

And time as it stands
Won't be held in my hands
Or living inside of my skin
And as it fell from the sky
I asked myself why
Can I never let anyone in?

I thought that I heard someone say now
There's no time for running away now
Hey now, hey now

Feel no shame
'Cause time's no chain
Feel no shame

Feel no shame
'Cause time's no chain
Feel no shame

I hitched a ride with my soul by the side of the road
Just as the sky turned black
I took a walk with my fame down memory lane
I never did find my way back

You know that I gotta say time's slippin' away
What will it hold for me?
What am I gonna do while I'm lookin' at you?
You're standing ignoring me

I thought that I heard someone say now
There's no time for running away now
Hey now, hey now, hey now
Hey now, hey now, hey now, hey now
Hey now, hey now, hey now
Feel no shame
'Cause time's no chain
Feel no shame
'Cause time's no chain

SOME MIGHT SAY

Some might say that sunshine follows thunder
Go and tell it to the man who cannot shine
Some might say that we should never ponder
On our thoughts today 'cause they hold sway over time

Some might say we will find a brighter day
Some might say we will find a brighter day

'Cause I've been standing at the station in need of education in the rain
You made no preparation for my reputation once again
The sink is full of fishes, she's got dirty dishes on the brain
It was overflowing gently, it's so elemen'try my friend

Some might say they don't believe in heaven
Go and tell it to the man who lives in hell
Some might say you get what you've been given
If you don't get yours I won't get mine as well

Some might say we will find a brighter day
Some might say we will find a brighter day

'Cause I've been standing at the station in need of education in the rain
You made no preparation for my reputation once again
The sink is full of fishes, she's got dirty dishes on the brain
And my dog's been itching, itching in the kitchen once again

Some might say, some might say
You know what some might say
You know what some might say

CAST NO SHADOW

Here's a thought for every man
Who tries to understand what is in his hands
He walks along the open road of love and life
Arriving if he can

Bound with all the weight of all the words he tried to say
Chained to all the places that he never wished to stay
Bound with all the weight of all the words he tried to say
As he faced the sun he cast no shadow

As they took his soul they stole his pride
As they took his soul they stole his pride
As they took his soul they stole his pride
As he faced the sun he cast no shadow

Here's a thought for every man
Who tries to understand what is in his hands
He walks along the open road of love and life
Arriving if he can

Bound with all the weight of all the words he tried to say
Chained to all the places that he never wished to stay
Bound with all the weight of all the words he tried to say
As he faced the sun he cast no shadow

As they took his soul they stole his pride
As they took his soul they stole his pride
As they took his soul they stole his pride
As they took his soul they stole his pride

As he faced the sun he cast no shadow
As he faced the sun he cast no shadow
As he faced the sun he cast no shadow

CHAMPAGNE SUPERNOVA

How many special people change?
How many lives are living strange?
Where were you while we were getting high?
Slowly walking down the hall, faster than a cannon ball
Where were you while we were getting high?
Some day you will find me caught beneath the landslide
In a Champagne Supernova in the sky
Some day you will find me caught beneath the landslide
In a Champagne Supernova, a Champagne Supernova in the sky

Wake up the dawn and ask her why
A dreamer dreams, she never dies
Wipe that tear away now from your eyes
Slowly walkin' down the hall, faster than a cannon ball
Where were you while we were getting high?

Some day you will find me caught beneath the landslide
In a Champagne Supernova in the sky
Some day you will find me caught beneath the landslide
In a Champagne Supernova, a Champagne Supernova

'Cause people believe that they're gonna get away from the summer
But you and I, we live and die
The world's still spinning round, we don't know why
Why, why, why, why

How many special people change?
How many lives are living strange?
Where were you while we were getting high?
Slowly walking down the hall, faster than a cannon ball
Where were you while we were getting high?

Some day you will find me caught beneath the landslide
In a Champagne Supernova in the sky
Some day you will find me caught beneath the landslide
In a Champagne Supernova, a Champagne Supernova

'Cause people believe that they're gonna get away from the summer
But you and I, we live and die
The world's still spinning round, we don't know why
Why, why, why, why

How many special people change?
How many lives are living strange?
Where were you when we were getting high?
We were getting high
We were getting high
We were getting high
We were getting high
We were getting high

SHE'S ELECTRIC

She's electric,
She's in a family full of eccentrics
She's done things I've never expected
And I need some time
She's got a sister
And God only knows how I've missed her
And on the palm of her hand is a blister
And I need more time

And I want you to know I've got my mind made up now
But I need more time

And I want you to say, do you know what I'm saying?
But I need more, 'cause I'll be you and you'll be me
There's lots and lots for us to see
Lots and lots for us to do
She is electric, can I be electric too?

She's got a brother
We don't get on with one another
But I quite fancy her mother
And I think that she likes me
She's got a cousin
In fact she's got 'bout a dozen
She's got one in the oven
But it's nothing to do with me

And I want you to know I've got my mind made up now
But I need more time

And I want you to say, do you know what I'm saying?
But I need more, 'cause I'll be you and you'll be me
There's lots and lots for us to see
Lots and lots for us to do
She is electric, can I be electric too?
Can I be electric too?
Can I be electric too?
Can I be electric too?

MORNING GLORY

All your dreams are made
When you're chained to the mirror with your razor blade
Today's the day that all the world will see
Another sunny afternoon
Walking to the sound of my favourite tune
Tomorrow never knows what it doesn't know too soon

Need a little time to wake up
Need a little time to wake up, wake up
Need a little time to wake up
Need a little time to rest your mind
You know you should, so I guess you might as well

What's the story, Morning Glory?
Well, you need a little time to wake up, wake up
Well, what's the story, Morning Glory?
Well, you need a little time to wake up, wake up

All your dreams are made
When you're chained to the mirror with your razor blade
Today's the day that all the world will see
Another sunny afternoon
Walking to the sound of my favourite tune
Tomorrow never knows what it doesn't know too soon

Need a little time to wake up
Need a little time to wake up, wake up
Need a little time to wake up
Need a little time to rest your mind
You know you should, so I guess you might as well

What's the story, Morning Glory?
Well, you need a little time to wake up, wake up
Well, what's the story, Morning Glory?
Well, you need a little time to wake up, wake up

Well, what's the story, Morning Glory?
Well, you need a little time to wake up, wake up
Well, what's the story, Morning Glory?
Well, you need a little time to wake up, wake up

Tablature & Instructions Explained

The tablature stave comprises six lines, each representing a string on the guitar as illustrated.

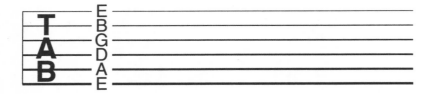

A number on any of the lines indicates, therefore, the string and fret on which a note should be played.

A useful hint to help you read tablature is to cut out small squares of self-adhesive paper and stick them on the upper edge of the guitar neck adjacent to each of the frets, numbering them accordingly. Be careful to use paper that will not damage the finish on your guitar.

Finger Vibrato

Tremolo Arm
Vibrato

Glissando

Strike the note, then slide
the finger up or down
the fretboard as indicated.

Tremolo Strumming

This sign indicates
fast up and down
stroke strumming.

8va

This sign indicates that
the notes are to be played an
octave higher than written.

loco

This instruction
cancels the above.

This note-head indicates
the string is to be totally muted
to produce a percussive effect.

P.M. = Palm mute

HALF TONE BEND

Play the note G then bend
the string so that the pitch rises
by a half tone (semi-tone).

FULL TONE BEND

DECORATIVE BEND

PRE-BEND

Bend the string as indicated,
strike the string and release.

GHOST NOTE

The note is half sounded

BEND & RELEASE

Strike the string, bend it as
indicated, then release the bend
whilst it is still sounding.

BEND & RESTRIKE

Strike the string, bend or gliss
as indicated, then restrike the
string where the symbol occurs.

UNISON BEND

Strike both strings
simultaneously then
immediately bend the
lower string as indicated.

STAGGERED UNISON BEND

Strike the lower string and bend as
indicated; whilst it is still sounding
strike the higher string.

HAMMER-ON

Hammer a finger down
on the next note without
striking the string again.

PULL-OFF

Pull your finger off the string
with a plucking motion to
sound the next note without
striking the string again.

RAKE-UP

Strum the notes upwards
in the manner of an
arpeggio.

RAKE-DOWN

Strum the notes downwards
in the manner of an
arpeggio.

HARMONICS

Strike the string whilst
touching it lightly at the
fret position shown.
Artificial Harmonics, (A.H.),
will be described in context.

Hello

Words & Music by Noel Gallagher

(includes extract from Hello, Hello, I'm Back Again - Words & Music by Gary Glitter & Mike Leander)

No - bo - dy e - ver men - tions the weath - er can make or break___ your day.___

No - bo - dy e - ver seems___ to re - mem - ber life is a game___ we play.___

We live___ in the sha - dows and___ we had the chance and threw it a - way.___

Let ring…   sim.

Chorus:

And it's ne - ver gon - na be the same,_____ 'cos the years

____ are fall - ing by_____ the rain.____ It's ne - ver gon - na be the same____

____ 'til the light____ by you____ comes to my____ house and says____ hel - lo.____

1.

2. There

2.

house and says: Hel - lo,

hel - lo. (It's good to be back, it's

Vocal tacet 2nd time

hel - lo,_____   hel - lo._____

Verse 2:
There ain't no sense in feeling lonely
They got no faith in you
But I've got a feeling you still owe me
So wipe the shit from your shoes.

Nobody ever mentions the weather *etc...*

Roll With It

Words & Music by Noel Gallagher

You got - ta roll____ with it, you got - ta take____ you time, you got - ta

C sus²   G/B   A sus⁴

say____ what you say,____ don't let an - y - bo - dy get in your way, 'cause it's all____ too much____ Hold... Hold...

G

____ for me to take.____ Don't e - ver

stand___ a - side, don't e - ver be de - nied, you wan - na be___ who you'd be___ if you're

com - in' with me.___ I think I've got a feel - in' I've lost___ in - side,___ I

Hold...   Hold...

think I'm gon - na take me a - way___ and___ hide,___ I'm think - in' of things___ that I___

Hold...   Hold...   Hold...   Hold...

D sus⁴ ... G

just can't a - bide. I

%% F ... G

know the roads down which your life will drive,

F

I'll find the key that lets you stop in - side.

Kiss___ the girl,___ she's not___

___ be - hind___ the door,_____ but you

know I think I rec - og - nise___ your face___ but I ne - ver seen you be - fore.

You got-ta roll___ with it, you got-ta

take___ your time, you got-ta say___ what you say,___ don't let an-y-bo-dy get in your way,

'cause it's all___ too much___ for me to take.___

19

Solo:
G

C add⁹   G/B   A sus⁴

C add⁹   G/B   A sus⁴   C add⁹   G/B   D sus⁴

Coda ⊕

Don't e - ver stand___ a - side, don't e - ver

be___ de - nied, you wan - na be___ who you'd be___ if you're com - in' with me.___

think I've got a feel-in' I've lost____ in - side,____ I

Hold...   Hold...

Fig.1...   ...end Fig.1.

1,2,3.   **4.**

think I've got a feel-in' I've lost____ in - side.____   I ____ in - side.____

sim.

Play 3 times   G

Solo gtr   Gliss   Gliss

w/Fig.1.

Gliss   Gliss

Wonderwall

Words & Music by Noel Gallagher

I don't be-lieve___ that an - y-bo - dy feels the way I do___ a-bout you now.___

Verse :

2. Back beat, the word is on the street that the fire___ in your heart is out,___
See Block Lyrics for Verse 3

CELLO

F♯   A   E   B

I'm sure you've heard it all be-fore but you ne-ver real-ly had a doubt.___

I don't be-lieve___ that an - y-bo-dy feels the way I do___ a-bout you now.___

___ And all___

B⁷sus⁴

Be - cause

Chorus:

D add⁹   F♯m⁷   A   F♯m

may - be _____ you're gon - na be the one that

Strum

D add⁹   F♯m   A   F♯m

saves   me, _____ and af - ter all _____

may - be_____ you're gon - na be the one that

saves me_____ and af - ter all,_____

you're my won - der - wall._____

I said

may - be you're gon - na be the one that

saves me, you're gon - na be the one that

Verse 3:
Today was gonna be the day
But they'll never throw it back to you
By now you should've somehow
Realised what you're not to do
I don't believe that anybody feels the way I do
About you now.

And all the roads that lead you there were winding
And all the lights that light the way are blinding
There are many things that I would like to say to you
But I don't know how.

Don't Look Back In Anger

Words & Music by Noel Gallagher

a bet-ter place to play._____

You said_____ that you_____ ne-ver been,_____ but all the things that you've seen_____

slow-ly fade a-way._____

So I start a re-vo-lu-tion from my bed, 'cause you said the brains I had went to my

head. Step out-side, Sum-mer-time's in bloom,

stand up be-side the fire - place,___ take that look from off___ your face,___ you ain't e - ver gon - na burn___ my

heart___ out.___ And

Chorus:

So Sal - ly can wait,___ she knows it's too late___ as we're walk - ing on by.___

Hold... *sim.*

Her soul slides a - way,___

but don't___ look back___ in an - ger, I heard you say.__

she knows it's too late _____ as we're walk - ing on by. _____

_____ Her soul slides a - way, _____

_____ but don't ___ look back ___ in an - ger, don't look back in an - ger, _____

I heard you say,_____

it's not too late.

Verse 2:
Take me to the place where you go
Where nobody knows if it's night or day
But please don't put your life in the hands
Of a rock 'n' roll band who'll throw it all away.

I'm gonna start a revolution from my bed
'Cause you said the brains I had went to my head
Step outside 'cause summertime's in bloom
Stand up beside the fireplace, take that look from off your face
'Cause you ain't never gonna burn my heart out.

Cast No Shadow

Words & Music by Noel Gallagher

☐ = downstroke

V = upstroke

Verse:

Here's a thought___ for ev - 'ry man___ who tries___ to un - der - stand___ what is in his hands..

He

walks a - long___ the o - pen road___ of love___ and life___ sur - viv - ing if he can.

Bound with all the weight___ of all___ the words___ he tried to say._____

Chained to all___ the plac - es that___ he ne - ver wished___ to stay._____

Bound with all___ the weight___ of all___ the words he tried to say._____

As he faced the sun he cast_____ no sha - dow.

Chorus:
G

As they took his soul_____

_____ they stole_____ his pride._____

Play 3 times

To Coda ⊕

As he faced the sun he cast_____

_____ no sha - dow._____

D.C. al ⊕ Coda
(with all repeats)

(Asus⁴)

Gliss

Gliss

⊕ Coda

As they took his soul _____

they took his pride.

As he faced the sun he cast

1,2,3.

no sha - dow,

Hey Now

Words & Music by Noel Gallagher

Chorus:

Verse 2:
The first thing I saw
As I walked through the door
Was a sign on the wall that read
It said you might never know
That I want you to know
What's written inside of your head.

And time as it stands
Won't be held in my hands
Or living inside of my skin
And as it fell from the sky
I asked myself why
Can I never let anyone in?

The Swamp Song

Words & Music by Noel Gallagher

...end Fig.1.

Solo:

Rhythm gtr continues Fig.1

Some Might Say

Words & Music by Noel Gallagher

sun - shine fol - lows thun - der,   go and tell___

___ it to___ the man___ who can - not shine.___

Some might say___ that we should ne - ver pon -

-der   on our thoughts____ to - day____ 'cause they____

____ hold sway____ o - ver time.____   Some might say____

Let ring…

Chorus:

____   we will find____ a bright - er day.____

Let ring…

Some might say   we will find   a bright - er day.

'Cause I've been stand - ing at the sta - tion   in

need of ed - u - ca - tion in the rain.   You

made no pre-pa-ra-tion for my re-pu-ta-tion once a-gain._____

The sink is full of fish-es, she's got dir-ty dish-es on the

brain._____ It was o-ver-flow-ing gent-ly,
2nd time: And my dog's been itch-ing,

68

Verse 2(𝄋):
She's got a brother
We don't get on with one another
But I quite fancy her mother
And I think that she likes me
She's got a cousin
In fact she's got 'bout a dozen
She's got one in the oven
But it's nothing to do with me.

The Swamp Song

Words & Music by Noel Gallagher

Morning Glory

Words & Music by Noel Gallagher

Em   D   A⁷sus⁴   Cadd⁹

day's the day___ that all___ the world___ will see.___

Em   D

An - oth - er sun - ny af - ter - noon,___

Em   D   Em   D

walk - ing to the sound of my fav - 'rite tune,___ to - mor - row ne - ver knows what it

up, wake ___ up. Well, _____

what's the sto - ry, Morn - ing Glo - ry? Well, _____

you need a lit - tle time to wake ___ up, wake ___ up.

what's the sto - ry, Morn - ing Glo - ry?

Well,_____ you need a lit - tle time to wake_____

_____ up, wake_____ up.

w/ad lib. solo

Champagne Supernova

Words & Music by Noel Gallagher

1. How ma-ny spe-cial peo-ple change?____ How ma-ny lives are liv-ing strange?____

Where were you___ while we were get-ting high?___

Slow-ly walk-ing down___ the hall,___ fast-er than___ a can-non ball,___

where were you___ while we were get-ting high?___ Some day you will

Chorus:

find me caught be - neath___ the land - slide,_____ in a Cham -

- pagne Su - per - no - va in the sky._____ Some - day you will

find me caught be - neath___ the land - slide,_____ in a Cham -

-pagne Su - per - no - va, a Cham - pagne Su - per - no - va in the sky.

Let ring...

mf
w/Fig.1.

Strum

sim.

Verse:

2. Wake up the dawn and ask her why, a dream-er dreams, she ne-ver dies,
See Block Lyrics for Verse 3

Fig.2...

wipe that tear a-way now from your eyes.

...end Fig.2.

Slow-ly walk-in' down the hall, fast-er than a can-non ball, where were you___ while we were get-ting high?___ Some day you will

Heavy

Chorus:

find me caught be-neath___ the land - slide,___ in a Cham-

- pagne Su-per-no - va in the sky.___ Some - day you will

find me caught be - neath___ the land - slide,_____ in a Cham -

- pagne Su - per - no - va, a Cham - pagne Su - per - no - va. 'Cause

Bridge:

peo - ple be - lieve___ that they're gon - na get a - way from the sum - mer.

But you and I,_____ we live and die,_____ the

world's still spin-ning round,___ we don't know why, why, why,___ why, why.

24/2/97

1.

Asus^2 /G   /F$\sharp$ /E

mf

w/Figs 1&2.

How ma - ny spe - cial peo - ple change?___ How ma - ny lives are liv - ing strange?___

Let ring... ⌐ Strum ⌐ *sim.*

Where were you___ when we were get - ting high?___ We were get - ting high.___

___ We were get - ting high,___ we were get - ting high,___

we were get-ting high,_____ we were get-ting high. _____
Vocal fades on repeat

Verse 3:
How many special people change?
How many lives are living strange?
Where were you while we were getting high?
Slowly walkin' down the hall
Faster than a cannonball
Where were you while we were getting high?

3/96 (23877)